India Travel Guide

Health Advice and Tips for Travelers to India

By

Shalu Sharma

Copyright:

Disclaimer:

Whilst every care is taken to ensure that the information in this book is as up-to-date and accurate as possible, no responsibility can be taken by the author for any errors or omissions contained herein. Responsibility for any loss, damage, accident or distress resulting from adherence to any advice, suggestions or recommendations is not taken.

ISBN-13: 978-1505380606
ISBN-10: 150538060X
CreateSpace Independent Publishing Platform, North Charleston, SC

Table of contents

1. Introduction to safe traveling in India

India is a country with a lot of great history and monumental sites to see. Because India is such a tourist attraction, people from the developed parts of the world might assume that they are perfectly safe traveling in India. Even though India does thrive on tourism for its economy, that doesn't mean all aspects of traveling within the country are safe. New tourists might not be prepared for how economically poor the country is. India is still considered a third world country, which means they have chronic problems with disease, crime and poverty throughout their land. Travelers need to take precautions before they perform everyday activities in the country, like eating at restaurants, walking on the streets and even breathing the air. Remember that you won't be able to just call 9-1-1 and have an ambulance take you to the hospital if you are feeling ill. India has a very poor healthcare system with a limited supply of medicine and treatments available. That is why it is crucial that you take care of your own health instead. The only way you can do this is by taking preventative action. Unless you are traveling with a doctor, you won't be able to have access to one if you get sick. This is something you need to think about for you and your family's sake before visiting India.

International Arrivals at the Indira Gandhi Airport, Delhi

Anytime you travel to a third world country like India, you will want to have travel health insurance. This is a special kind of health insurance that is temporary and covers you throughout the duration of your scheduled itinerary. You would be amazed how many travelers just assume that their regular health insurance plans from their native country will cover them. Whether you are from a country with socialized medicine or a country where you pay a healthcare premium, none of that will matter if you don't get sick in that country. Even if you somehow fly back to your native country after obtaining an illness in India, chances are your healthcare plan won't cover you because you got sick on foreign soil. Therefore, make sure you research travel health insurance plans where you specify to the sales agent exactly where you are going on your trip and what you will be doing. You will want your policy to cover all the possible illnesses that you could obtain on your trip, like yellow fever, malaria and even rabies. Of course, you should still take preventive measures to decrease your likelihood of getting these illnesses. Those will be discussed later in this book. But, travel health insurance is always a good thing to have because you never know what can happen to you in a foreign country that you are not familiar with.

Inside the complex of Agra Fort, Agra

Let this book act as a guide for keeping you healthy and safe during your trip to India. It is not meant to scare or deter you from traveling to the country. Instead, it just takes into account all of the realistic problems that could arise when you are there and the ways you can prevent them from happening. After all, it is better to be safe than sorry. India is a beautiful country with a lot of fine restaurants and monuments, but it also has its share of problems as well. Tourists need to be aware of those problems, so that they don't fall into a deadly trap that they can't get out of. By following the advice in this book, you will allow yourself and your family to have a happy and safe trip without the worries of getting sick or dying from a terrible disease.

2. Deep Vein Thrombosis on long haul flights and how to prevent it

Deep vein thrombosis, or DVT, is a problem that many travelers face when they go on long flights. It is basically a blood clot that will form in the deep vein of your leg after staying immobile for extended periods of time. What happens is the blood flow in your leg moves slowly when you aren't moving around. If the blood moves too slowly then it could form a clot after awhile. If you are a westerner going on a flight to India, you will probably be sitting for around 18 hours or more. This would definitely put you at risk of getting a blood clot because all it takes is for a person to be immobile for only four hours before they are at risk of getting DVT. There isn't much you can do about it while you're on the plane because you have to stay seated for most of the time. You could occasionally get up to go to the bathroom every couple hours to stretch your legs. This could help tremendously in getting blood flow moving faster in your legs. Then while you are seated, you could do a series of leg exercises that involve bending and straightening your legs. Try to have as much room as possible in front of you. This means avoid putting your carryon bags on the floor in front of you. Another trick to increase blood flow is to press your feet down hard on the floor. You can do this at any time if you start to feel numb in your legs.

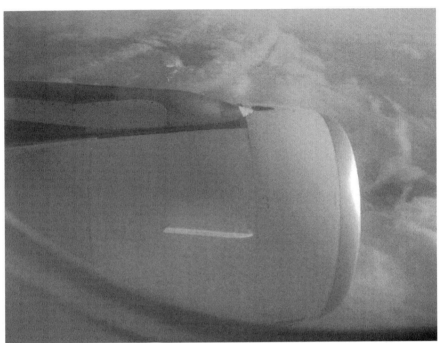
Long hours traveling to India

If you have a pair of elastic compression stockings then you might want to wear them on your legs before the trip. There has been scientific evidence that shows these stockings have helped people who have a high risk of getting DVT. These stockings can be purchased at pharmacies. Make sure you tell your pharmacist that you want "graduated compression" in your stockings that go up to your knee. This will help prevent blood clotting, but it won't totally prevent it. You still have to stretch your legs and move around as often as you can in addition to wearing them. Besides this, you should be wary of what you ingest into your system while sitting. The food and drinks that you have on the plane could possibly contribute to DVT. You will want to avoid drinking alcohol because that causes immobility and dehydration. You should also avoid sleeping tablets because they will make you immobile as well. Instead, drink plenty of water to stay hydrated because this will help the blood flow stay active.

Those suffering from Deep vein thrombosis should avoid alcohol if they can

For people who have an extremely high risk of getting DVT, you may want to get an injection of heparin from your doctor before the trip. Heparin is basically a blood thinner that will help prevent clots from forming in your legs. You should also see your doctor if you have cancer or have had a major surgery recently. These things will increase your risk of getting DVT as well. What you should not do is take aspirin to prevent clotting in the leg. Aspirin prevents clots in the arteries of your heart, but not in the veins of your leg. So, stick with these other methods that were discussed and you should be able to avoid getting DVT. Chances are if you are already in good physical shape, meaning you exercise regularly, then your body should be able to endure one long 18 hour trip. It is those people who are normally out of shape that tend to pose the biggest risk of getting DVT. They are the ones that need to take the most precautions.

3. Vaccinations for India

When you start to plan your trip to go to India, it would definitely be a good idea to make an appointment with a doctor and get a vaccination prior to going. This might sound a little extreme for a vacation or trip, but you have to remember that sickness can be obtained much easier there. The Center for Disease Control recommends that people get their immunizations about six weeks in advance before arriving in India. The vaccinations that you receive will take about that long before they take full effect in your body. As for the types of vaccinations you'll want to have those that all coincide with the diseases that are prevalent in India. These diseases commonly found in India are Hepatitis A, Hepatitis B, Typhoid fever, Japanese Encephalitis, rabies, Cholera and yellow fever. Most of these diseases exist in rural areas, but you may still come in contact with a person or contaminated food that carries the disease.

Rajgir in Bihar, a popular Buddhist destination

Hepatitis A and Typhoid fever can be contracted through food and water contamination, which is very common in India. Hepatitis B is more of a viral infection that can be transmitted to other people through the transfer of bodily fluids. This can occur in sexual activity, accidents and even medical care at an Indian hospital. For diseases like Japanese encephalitis and yellow fever, these are diseases that can be obtained just from getting bit by a mosquito. This is something you really can't avoid because mosquitoes are everywhere in India. Plus, if you spend a lot of time outside then you are likely to come across animals that have rabies. Therefore, there are a lot of diseases and illnesses to worry about when going to India. In fact, the one vaccination that is actually mandatory for tourists to receive is the one for yellow fever. When you arrive in India, you may be asked to show proof that you have received a vaccination for yellow fever depending where you have been traveling to. This usually happens when they check your passport and find that you have been to a country in the past that is prone to yellow fever. So, they make sure you have a vaccination as a precaution so that you don't possibly spread yellow fever or obtain it. If you don't show this proof then it is possible for the Indian government to quarantine you for about a week before they let you go.

You may be wondering if you need vaccinations for every single one of these diseases. Well, that is really up to your healthcare provider to determine. Before any vaccinations are given out, your doctor will first give you a medical checkup and review your health history. They will especially look into any past immunization treatments and the health effects they had on your body. They may require you to have your U.S. vaccinations up to date for things like polio, mumps, measles, chickenpox and diphtheria. Some doctors may also want to review your itinerary for India and determine which diseases you are most likely to come in close contact with based on your planned activities there. Once all of this has been determined, the doctor will suggest the vaccinations that you should need prior to going to India. You may feel some mild side effects from the vaccinations, which is perfectly natural if you have never had them before. Some of these side effects may be flu-like symptoms, such as runny nose, coughing and congestion. These are mild symptoms that will pass after your body has had a chance to absorb the chemicals from the vaccination. By the time your trip comes along, you should be all set and ready to travel without any more negative symptoms.

Must have vaccinations include Hepatitis A, Tetanus, Typhoid and Cholera while you should consider Diphtheria, Hepatitis B, Japanese Encephalitis and Rabies.

4. Restaurant and food guide for India

India has a lot of fine restaurants with exotic cuisine that tastes great. Tourists should embrace the cultural differences in the food choices and not be afraid to try new things. Of course, you still have to be cautious when choosing a restaurant and eating food from there. You have to remember that India does not have all the health and sanitary codes that more developed countries have, like the United States. In that country, restaurants have all got to meet a certain set of health requirements for the establishment. If they don't then they are out of business. Indian restaurants are not like that, so you need to know what to look for in order to prevent yourself from getting sick.

Chow mein, although Chinese this dish is very popular in India

The best way to stay healthy in India is to be sanitary with everything. This means washing your hands before and after every meal that you eat there. But, don't just go to the bathroom and rinse your hands under the faucet in the sink because you don't know what kinds of germs exist in the water supply. Instead, you just have a vast supply of hand wipes with an antibacterial ingredient called "benzalkonium chloride." You can also go with a hand sanitizer that has this ingredient as well. Use whichever one you feel is more comfortable to carry around with you on your trip. Of course, this only cleans your skin and hands from germs that are on the outside of your body. If you eat food that is contaminated or diseased then that is a whole other problem right there. You won't always know if the food is diseased either. All you can do is take precautions for when you choose a restaurant or a specific meal. The first thing you should remember is to never pick a restaurant that has nobody else eating there. Chances are the word has gotten out around town that something is not right about that particular establishment. Perhaps, the food is not fresh and has a reputation for making people sick. Next, you should only order meals that are extremely hot because the hot temperature can kill most germs and bacteria that may be on the food. Therefore, avoid foods that are cold or lukewarm. Also, try to only drink beverages that come out of a can or bottle because the glasses are not always washed thoroughly in some restaurants. As for the plates, if you suspect that they are not clean, you can always wipe them off the best you can before your meal is served. Don't use the hand wipes, but rather a clean towel that you brought with you. However, in most good restaurants, you won't have to.

You will know if a restaurant is clean or not

If you are a westerner then you might get tempted to order some westernized Indian food, like pizza and hamburgers. Don't do this in local Indian restaurants because Indian locals don't eat this kind of food. That means the food likely won't be fresh. If you need to eat a westernized meal then do it at major hotels and restaurants only because they are tourist attractions and are often ordered by other tourists. As a matter of fact, try to always eat in bigger restaurants that have a lot of people. This means physical establishments with a big staff and clean eating areas. Chances are the food is healthy in a place like this or else there would be a lot of sick people coming back to complain. Now whatever you do, do not eat any street food. You will find a lot of street vendors selling food on their tables, but there are no guarantees how clean or well cooked the food actually is. For all you know, the food could have been sitting outside for days and has likely rotted or been contaminated.

To sum everything up, eat at big restaurants and stay as sanitary as possible. Wipe down the silverware, plates and your hands. Try to drink from cans or bottles. If you do these things then you will have a good chance of avoiding sickness.

5. Traveler's diarrhea and how to avoid it

Traveler's diarrhea is a term that describes when a person gets infected with bacteria that makes them endure stomach pains and loose stools. You may even endure fever, vomiting and nausea in addition to this. Traveler's diarrhea is basically a digestive tract disorder that you get from drinking contaminated water or eating foods that are contaminated. The bacterium that causes this is called "escherichia coli," which basically attaches itself to the inner lining of the intestines and then releases toxins that cause the symptoms. In India, this disorder has been nicknamed Delhi Belly because a lot of people obtain this problem from eating Indian food in the city of Delhi. On the plus side, this is not some fatal disorder that is going to kill you or leave you greatly ill. It is simply an unpleasant disorder that will have you in pain or running to the bathroom every five minutes during your trip. Whether you are on vacation or there for business, you probably want to enjoy yourself as much as possible without worrying about stomach issues. So, the best thing you can do is take preventive action to avoid getting the bacteria inside of you that causes this disorder.

What can you say about this street food? Most of the food is open and chances are that you might get diarrhea if you had it

When you travel to India, chances are you are going to eat the native food that is cooked and is available. After all, part of the fun of traveling is to try exotic cuisine prepared by other cultures. However, you still have to be cautious in India because of all the unsanitary conditions that may exist in some restaurants. This goes back to the previous chapter for the restaurant and food guide. You will only want to drink water out of sealed bottles because water from a supply tap might be contaminated. Even locals drink bottled water when they are out and about.

As for the food, make sure you order hot meals because heat can kill bacteria that may exist on the food. This is really the best you can do because you don't really know for sure what is on the food until after you eat it. If you are really worried then you can always pack your own preserved food to eat on the trip. This would be good advice for people with weaker immune systems because they are more vulnerable to infections. If not, then simply be careful where you eat.

Carry bottled water with you. You can buy them everywhere even on small stalls

There are a few preventive treatments that you can give yourself to reduce the risk of getting infected with the bacteria that causes Delhi Belly. Believe it or not, antacids can actually kill the microorganisms of the bacteria that are in your stomach. You could buy a simple over-the-counter treatment, like TUMS, to help do this. Just take a few chewable tablets after you eat at an Indian restaurant and it will reduce your chances of getting Delhi Belly. But please, don't think of this as a license to just eat carelessly without taking into consideration where and what you are eating. It will simply reduce your chances of getting the illness, but it won't completely prevent it. In addition, drink plenty of fruit juices from a can or cartons. The antioxidants will help clean out your system of toxins. You should also avoid drinking anything caffeinated or that comes from dairy products because this will dehydrate you even more in case you get the illness.

However, if you notice that you have symptoms of Delhi Belly and they are not going away after about a week, then you should definitely see a physician. They will prescribe you antibiotics or may even recommend that you take Pepto-bismol, considering how bad the symptoms are. If you are in India then you may be able to find the Pepto-bismol in some shops in India but cannot guarantee it, but you should wait on the antibiotics until you get back to your native country. An alternative herbal medicine called Pudin Hara in liquid and tablet form is available in India and considered very good for soothing the stomach.

Besides all this, just continue to drink plenty of fluids and even green tea if you can get it. This will all help wash the infection out of your system like any other flu or cold.

6. Bottled water guide

One of the most important things you can do while in India is buy bottled or packaged water. Whatever you do, don't drink out of the tap. It's not that it is going to be dirty and all tap water in India is contaminated, it's just that you don't know if it's going to suit you or not. So just buy bottled water in India. Drinks such as soda, juices and other drinks in the market will be alright but try not to drink water from the tap at your hotel.

There are two types of bottled water categories in India namely: Packaged drinking water and Natural mineral water (spring water). Most of the water sold in bottles is packaged drinking water that has been purified and is cheaper while the mineral water is little more expensive. They both are equally safe. International tourists prefer to buy mineral water rather than the packaged water. These waters can range from 15 Rupees for the cheaper variations to 50 Rupees for the more expensive ones.

There are 200 bottled water brands to choose from and most of them are local. The most popular is Bisleri. Other popular ones include Kinely, Himalayan, Bailey's, Kingfisher Mineral Water and Aquafina. They are available almost everywhere from railway platforms to little stalls outside tourist places. You will even find people coming up to you and try to sell you water.

There are a few things to remember when buying these bottles of water. Sometimes, bottles are filled with tap water and sold off as packed water. India is a developing country and even though there are tough regulations, some unscrupulous individuals and even gangs try to make money by selling fake things including water. To the casual buyer, they may not even know that they are buying tap water. However, there are a few things you can check to figure out if you are buying the real thing or not.

Kinley is one of the popular brands. Not all restaurants and shops will have all the brands

First let's look at some alternatives.

You can avoid drinking water all together and drink cola, cartoned drinks and fruit juices. Since packed drinks such as Coke, Pepsi and other drinks that come in cans and cartons are branded products and it's more difficult to fake them.

When you order food, ask for a bottle of mineral or packaged water as well. Don't drink out of the tap even at the hotel

You can always boil water and take them with you. Most hotels will have kettles or you can bring your own travel kettle with you and boil water from the tap or packaged water and refill the bottles and take them with you.

Carry a mini water purifier. There are some purifiers that come in the size of a pen and you can purify the water in minutes.

But the most convenient thing is to buy bottled water. Here is a trick you can use to identify a fake water bottle. Buy a bottle and open it with your ears to the cap. It should make some clicking sound when the seal is broken. If it's fake then it will not make as much it should and will open with relative ease. Although this is a not a fool proof method, but we all know that when opening a new bottle of water, it should make some snapping sound and if it doesn't then it indicates that something has been tampered or simply glued back on.

This may not be the best solution but you could buy bottled water at reputed sources such as your hotel and shops. This will ensure that the ones you are buying are not fake. Always go for the best water which includes Bisleri, Aquafina and Kinley. Make sure there is nothing floating in the water. Remember when you ask for mineral water, most shopkeepers will give you any bottled water that they might have stocked in their shop. If you are looking for the top brands, ask for them.

7. Malaria in India and how to prevent it

Malaria is a blood disease that transfers deadly parasites into your blood stream and then eventually kills you. Humans can obtain this disease from getting bitten by mosquitoes that are carrying it. Once the mosquito bites you, the parasites from the mosquito get underneath your skin and then inside of your blood. This is not some rare disease either. On a worldwide scale, there have been over 200 million cases reported of people being infected with malaria. Out of those 200 million cases there have been 800,000 deaths. Malaria typically exists throughout the southern hemisphere of the Earth, in regions like South America, the Middle East and Southern Asia where India lies. It is most deadly to pregnant women and young children because their immune systems are not strong enough to withstand the effects of the disease. That is why if you are traveling to India with your whole family then you need to make sure everybody has taken the proper precautions to avoid getting an infection with this disease.

Some places have lots of stagnant water – a source of mosquitoes to breed

The first step you should take is going to a physician and talking with them about drugs that can help prevent catching malaria. There are actually anti-malarial prescription drugs that a doctor can prescribe you, but they are not 100% effective in preventing the disease from infecting you. Just ask your doctor about malaria prophylaxis medications and they will know what you are talking about. It may also be a good idea for you to research the drug on your own because it does have some strong side effects that might interfere with your trip. These side effects include violent mood swings and depression. There are also some anti-malaria medications, like chloroquine, that have high resistance levels. Your doctor will know the right kind of anti-malaria medication to prescribe you after they know the areas of India you are traveling in. You should start taking your prescribed medicine at least 2 weeks prior to going to India. If a child is being prescribed this medication then they will have to take very small doses. It is always advised that children under 12 years of age should not travel to India because they are more prone to getting malaria and the preventive drugs won't be as effective for them.

Whether you are an adult or child, anti-malaria medications alone won't protect you completely from malaria. You should also try to avoid getting bit by mosquitoes all together since they are the reason for getting it in the first place. A good way to do this is to spray insect repellent on your skin. There are insect repellent mosquito gels and sprays you can buy in your local pharmacy.

Make sure you spray it on exposed skin and not skin covered with clothing. This is the most effective ingredient to deter mosquitoes away. Some repellents are even safe to apply on the skin of pregnant woman and children as well. You can get this repellent in other forms besides a spray bottle, like lotions and liquid. Of course, remember not to apply the repellent to open wounds in the skin because that will cause a stinging sensation and possibly other negative health effects. Also, don't press your luck by wearing shorts and a sleeveless shirt. Try to wear as much protective clothing as possible when you visit India because the more skin that is covered up, the less chances you give a mosquito to bite you. Finally, try to stay inside at nighttime. Female mosquitoes love to feed at nighttime, so you should stay in your hotel after dusk.
For the best protection, by a repellent spray that has the chemical DEET (N-diethyl-meta-toluamide) in it.

Other ways to prevent mosquitoes is to wear full sleeved clothing and using mosquito wrist bands. These mosquito bands release vapor through your body movement and form an anti-mosquito halo around you.

8. Dengue Fever in India and how to prevent it

Dengue fever is definitely a disease to watch out for in India. A human can get it by obtaining a virus from a mosquito that carries it around, usually an Aedes mosquito. You will know when you have the disease because you will experience some nasty symptoms like joint pain, muscle pain, eye pain, headaches, fever and a rash. Dengue fever is usually just a minor illness, but it can become fatal for some people that experience internal bleeding from it. That is why it is best to just take preventive actions, so that you don't have to find out the hard way what this disease will do to you. First, you must learn about the source of what you are dealing with.

In Delhi, Dengue fever jumps during the rainy season between the months of July and September

Aedes mosquitoes are the most common type of mosquito to carry and spread dengue. These mosquitoes often breed near water containers like barrels, flower pots, containers and even discarded tires. So, you will want to stay away from any watery areas or else you could risk getting bit by them. Also, you should be aware of the most active times that these mosquitoes will bite you. Shaded areas tend to have mosquitoes that will bite you any time of day. For the most part, they tend to fly around a lot for a few hours after dawn and before dusk. Therefore, if you are in a dry sunny area at around noon then you will have the least chance of getting bit and contracting dengue. All of this advice should be taken no matter if you are in an urban setting or a rural setting because Aedes mosquitoes inhabit both types of environments.

All tourists to India should have an insect repellent with them. To ward off Aedes mosquitoes you will need a repellent with at least 30% DEET, or N-diethyl-m-toluamide, and 15% picaridin. If you use a repellent with less DEET in it then you will have to apply the repellent more often. Since Aedes mosquitoes can bite you indoors as well as outdoors, you will need to have the repellent actively on you all the time when you are in India. Also, wear clothes that are long sleeved in order to reduce the amount of exposed skin. If your repellent has an ingredient called permethrin, then you can spray it on your clothes instead of your skin. Either way, if you are traveling with an infant to India then you should use a mosquito net on their baby carriage instead of repellent. Of course, it is not recommended that you travel with a child this small when visiting the country. But if you must go, use netting instead of a repellent because a repellent will make them sick. As for adults, they should stay in hotels that have screened windows. You may think that all hotels would automatically be screened, but there are some lesser class hotels in India that don't use them. If you are staying at a big hotel then it likely has air conditioning and so mosquitoes should not be an issue.

You may be wondering about vaccines that can prevent dengue fever. Unfortunately, there are no vaccines available for this condition. Furthermore, there is no medicine to treat or cure the illness either. A person that obtains dengue fever will only be given simple medicines by a doctor, like acetaminophen, to reduce their feverish symptoms. They may also be given plenty of fluids to rehydrate themselves and other blood pressure treatments. Dengue fever should eventually go away in time by drinking plenty of fluids, but you will still have to endure the uncomfortable feelings that it provides. The best thing is to take precautions in order to avoid getting it all together.

9. Air pollution in India and to avoid it

Air pollution is certainly a massive problem in some parts of India particularly the capital of India. Besides all of the heavy traffic emitting carbon into the air, you also have biomass burning, fuel wood burning and fuel adulteration problems as well. As a tourist in India, you can expect to see lots of air pollution in big cities, like Delhi. In fact, the World Health Organization recently named India as the worst air polluted country in the world, with Delhi being the worst polluted city. Any tourist will be able to tell that air pollution exists as soon as their plane lands. They will see the clouds of smog and dust throughout the city streets and beyond. As you probably know, air pollution can have many harmful effects on your lungs. It basically has the same negative effect as smoking tobacco, but at an increasingly harmful rate. You could walk three blocks in Delhi and the air pollution you inhale would do as much damage to your lungs as a pack of cigarettes. That should give you some idea how bad it is to breathe the air into your lungs.

Air pollution can be an issue for some travelers to India

Tourists might find the air pollution to be the biggest deterrent, besides all the diseases. However, there are not many safety measures you can take while in India to prevent yourself from inhaling too much polluted air. There is nothing much you can do about the air-pollution. Many Indians simply tend to cover their nose and mouth with handkerchief.

Basically, the handkerchief will act as a filter for the air you breathe in. It won't totally block the carbon and noxious elements from getting into your lungs, but it will reduce the percentage of them and prevent dust particles getting in your system. There are also more sophisticated masks you can buy, which are called "masks for air pollution or pollution masks". They seem to be very popular in the Far East and I have not seen anyone wear them in India.

Another type is the respirator mask which is basically a more technical version of the surgical mask because it contains an air purifier inside the mask that cleans the air before it releases it into your mouth. These kinds of masks you will have to bring with you before going to India. Even if you only want to use a surgical mask, bring those with you before going to India as well. The last thing you'll want to do is buy a mask from a street vendor because you won't know how new they really are. If you end up buying a used mask then you could catch germs or disease from the prior person who wore the mask. Therefore, buy your face masks ahead of time before going to India.

...But to be honest, putting masks will look awkward and you will stand out of the crowd...

You can always cover your face with a handkerchief

There is no true way to avoid air pollution all together. A country would have to stop emitting carbon into the air to really get rid of it, but don't count on that to ever happen. When you go to India, all you can do is protect yourself from the pollution the best you can. Other than that, there is nothing much you can do. This means eat and sleep indoors which is not possible if you are on holiday. Also, buy a portable air purifier and bring it with you. They make some purifiers small enough now to where you can actually wear them around your neck. This won't really protect you when you're outside, but it may be able to handle the smaller amounts of pollution that exist indoors. Again, it won't completely keep your lungs clean and safe, but it will reduce the possible damage it could cause to them. Also, if you are a smoker then try to refrain from smoking tobacco while in India. You don't want to mistreat your lungs anymore than you already have to.

10. Rabies in India and how to protect yourself

Rabies is a deadly viral disease that infects a person's nervous system. It is usually contracted from getting bit by another living organism that has rabies, such as a dog or bat. India has an ongoing problem with rabies throughout the country, especially its rural areas. These are the areas of India that have wild animals, bats and other creatures with rabies. All a person has to do is travel to one of these rural areas and they will likely encounter a rabid animal like bats and stray dogs. According to WHO, 36% of the world's rabies cases occur in India and three quarters of these are in the rural areas of India.

Street dogs are a common sight in many areas. In fact, this is a meat shop. Meat is sold openly in most parts of India

Rabies may be something easily dealt with in developed countries, like the United States, but in India you have to be extra careful. Please remember that there is no cure for rabies once the signs and symptoms of it are present inside a mammal. The only hope a person has is to keep vaccinated prior to getting infected or at the very least, getting vaccinated immediately after getting infected. In such a case, you will have to go to a hospital or a private clinic so the best thing is that you get the vaccinations in your own country before going there. If you end up getting bit on your trip, you should immediately scrub and rinse off the wound as thoroughly as you can. Then pour some alcohol or antiseptic on the open wound to disinfect it. After that, contact your travel insurance company immediately and let them know what is going on.

Hopefully, you purchased travel health insurance because they will pay for the vaccinations when you go back home or make sure they take you to a clinic where you will be given jabs. Either way, you should get back to your native country as soon as possible to continue getting vaccinated. You will need at least three more doses over the next three weeks to stop the disease from spreading.

If you get bit without a vaccination in your system, then you will need something else in addition to the standard vaccination. You will need something called rabies immunoglobulin, which is a very expensive treatment. So, it is always best to get vaccinated before risking the chance of getting bit. Also, the saliva of a rabid animal can still infect you if it gets into an open wound or absorbs through your skin. You should always take common sense steps to avoid being around wild and stray animals like dogs all together in the first place. Try to stay in the central touristy areas of India because there is less of a chance of getting bit by a rabid animal there. Just to be on the safe side, stay away from all dogs even if they look cute. You should also stay away from bats, raccoons, skunks and foxes, because they are the most common carriers of rabies. Sometimes the signs of a rabid animal might not be noticeable, but you should still take precautions around all animals in India because you never know.

Dogs along with cows at a garbage dump

The final piece of advice is to stay in a group when you travel around India. Chances are if one person gets bit, the others can fight off the animal and then treat your wound the best way possible. You have to remember that rabid animals are unnaturally aggressive, so they might try to just kill you all together. That is why you don't want to be alone in your travels. But, you should be fine as long as you take the advice given to you in this chapter. By getting vaccinated before your trip and then staying in touristy areas, you should not encounter any problems associated with rabies. In fact, tourists getting infected with rabies are rare because most of them stay around in and around the big cities anyways. You should apply the same concept to your travels.

11. Eating Indian street food safely

One of the great things about traveling to India is getting to try the different varieties of street food India has to offer. Some people would advice against eating street food completely, while some would advise you to try certain things but at the same time keeping an eye on the hygiene conditions of the vendor. My advice to foreign travellers particularly those who are coming from more cleaner countries to do exactly that which is try the various street food but with some caution.

First let's take a look at some of the types of Indian street food that is available on the streets. The most common Indian street food is the "chaat". This is a great dish and you will find them not just on the streets but also on the restaurant menu. There are different types of chaats but most usually the chaat will consist of chickpeas, samosas, chopped onions, ginger, chillies, noodles (called sev), yogurt, and tamarind sauce with lots of spices. The chaat is an old time favorite street food for the Indians and you will find many Indians eating chaat on the road side.

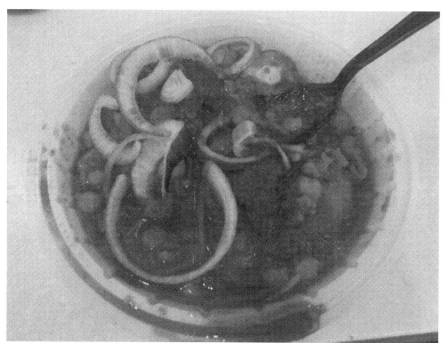
A plate of chaat, one of India's most popular street foods

The "gol guppa" (also called pani-puri) comes next in popularity. These are spicy water-filled dumplings. An absolutely delight! When you ask for a plate from the vendor, he will give you an empty plate and fill one of the gol-guppa with spicy water and put it the plate and you will have to put it in your mouth. By the time you finish one, the vendor would have given you another one. In addition other street foods would be masala dosa, samosa, pav bhaji, vada pav, egg roll and a host of others depending on where you are traveling in India.

Here's a guide to safety eating street food

Firstly, allow yourself a few days time to adjust to the climate of India. The conditions are harsh and you will find the place somewhat dusty depending on which part you are traveling.

So give yourself time to "climatise" and adjust to the local food. This will kind of prepare your body.

Make sure that the street food you want to have is covered in a glass container or cabinet. Indian roads can be very dusty and there could be lots of flies around the food cart. If you feel that the food is covered appropriately then the vendor has good hygiene practice and you could try the food being sold. In addition, just take a quick look at the plates and the utensils used to prepare the food along with the oil in which the food is being fried. If they are dirty, if there are insects like flies around them and they look dodgy then do not try them.

This stall selling a special dish called "Litti" seems OK. Have a quick look around and judge for yourself. If you feel everything hygienic then try it out.

If there are a lot of people around a particular vendor, this usually means that the food they are selling is perhaps very tasty. This doesn't automatically mean they are safe, it just means that the vendor might have a good reputation as far as the taste is concerned. Now if there are lots of families around with children, this means that they food they are selling is somewhat safe. I am very particular with my own children. I make sure if they do eat street food then the vendor has good clean plates and are prepared hygienically. One of the cooking techniques, Indian street food vendors use is to half fry the snacks and then refry them when you order. This is fine and re-frying will kill any germs.

If you see carts that are selling freshly squeezed fruit juices then you should demand to see the jug in which the squeezed juice is collected. If they do have anything in them then ask them to remove it before squeezing fresh juice. You can carry your own glass or thermos if you like and ask them to fill it up with juice.

Not strictly street food but this kiosk is better for a quick snack and a drink

Try to avoid street food that has meat in it unless you know that place very well and has a reputation.

Whatever you do, don't drink the water that is offered by the vendor. Always buy and drink bottled water. There are no golden rules, you are the best judge. Go by instinct. If you think you can cope, have a strong stomach and have had your vaccinations then by all means try them.

12. How to be gluten free in India?

We all love holidays and want to have a good time and try different things to eat. For most this is fine but for some they have to take care of what they eat. For those who are celiacs will have to take particular care of themselves. Since India will be a country where the language would be a barrier those traveling will have to be extra careful. Many people in India will not know what celiac is and awareness about celiac disease is extremely poor in India. In addition, sensitivity to gluten is often not recognised in this part of the word.

The chicken curry. If you find a good restaurant to eat, you can try curries including the chicken curry with rice

Another issue with India is that there is very little labelling on food packets and most of the time you will not know what the food contains. For instance, if you were to buy a packet of biscuits, it might just say that it contains starch and we know that starch is derived from wheat.

One great thing about Indian food is that there are lots of naturally gluten-free dishes. In fact, Indian restaurants are great to order gluten-free foods. But you should ideally confirm if they are wheat-free before ordering from the menu. There will always be someone who will speak English very well. If there is a language barrier, just ask to speak to someone who knows English well. If not, then one of the customers could always help out.

So let's take a look at what you can eat and choose those no-gluten containing ingredients while you are in India.

Here are some gluten-free Indian foods:

Tandoori chicken, chicken tikka masala, chicken or lamb curry and with most meat dishes
Fish dishes are almost always gluten-free
Most vegetable side dishes
Palak panner
Bhindi (okra or ladies finger) masala and other dishes made from this vegetable
Most veggie curries
Channa masala
Saag or palak (spinach) dishes
Rice and rice-based dishes
Biryani (chicken or lamb biryani)
Kebabs
Paneer tikka (made of homemade cheese)
Paneer makhani
Bajra Roti or Makki ki Roti (they are chapattis made of millet
Poha – Made of flattened rice, you'll find this being served as breakfast in many hotels and guest houses
Pulao – Made of rice and vegetables (similar to the biryani)

Dal – These are lentils and will be yellow in appearance. It goes well with rice.
Lassi – Yogurt based drink

Papadums (called papar in Hindi) are a crisp disk shaped type of flatbread made mainly lentils is fine. They are mainly made with lentils. For starters you can try the pakoras which are mainly made of vegetables battered with chickpea flour.

The Masala Dosa is a very popular in India and is made of rice, so this is one dish you can eat and is available in most restaurants. Side dishes that go with the masala dosa include coconut chutney and sambar made of vegetables and lentils. However, one type of dosa called the Rava dosa is made of wheat so be careful.

A plate of "Masala Dosa". You will find this dish in almost all restaurants

Having said all this, it is possible for food to be contaminated with wheat products. In addition, the same oil could be used to fry both wheat and non-wheat products. For instance samosas made of wheat could be fried in the same oil as the pakoras which are non-wheat products. So you need to ask and check what exactly they are doing if you are very sensitive.

List of things to avoid. Please remember this is not a complete list but list of popular items available in India that you should avoid as a celiac.

Chapattis, breads rolls, naan, parathas, puris
A spice called "asafoetida" or hing in Hindi and used in many wheat-based recipes in India such as hing-kachori.
Kachori are snacks made of wheat.
Samosas
Pav Bhaji – a popular snack made of vegetables and bun like bread.
Dal Baati Churma – Deep fried lentil-filled wheat balls served with chutney
Most Indian sweets

Beware of dishes with "maida flour" and with Suji (semolina), which actually contains wheat. One particular dish called Halva is made of suji which should be avoided.

Chapattis (called roti in Hindi) is also very popular and is a staple food in India but again you will need to avoid it as it's **made of wheat**. Variations of the chapatti include naan, puri, parathas and batura.

If you have a sweet tooth then you are in bad luck. Most Indian sweets will have some kind of wheat added to it. The best advice I can give you is to avoid Indian sweets. Sweets such as barfis, gulab jamun, rasgullas and jalebis will contain maida or wheat.

हमे कोलीयेक नमक बीमारी है. मुझे गेहू या आटा (ग्लूटेन) खाना माना है.
अगर आप को मालूम है की एस खाने मे क्या है, तो हमे बता दे.
हम सिर्फ़ चावल, मक्के, आलू, सब्जी, फल, आंडा, मछली खा सकते है.
मुझे आटा, गेहू, मयदा, खाना माना है.
क्या आप बता सकते है की एस खाने मे क्या है.
आप की सहायता के लिए धन्यवाद.

If you are having communication issues then you can show someone the above image who can read Hindi. The Hindi text translates as follows.

I have celiac disease and you cannot eat wheat (gluten).
If you know what this food contains then can you tell me
I can only eat rice, maize, potatoes, vegetables, fruits, eggs, fish.
I cannot eat wheat or flour.
Can you tell me what his food contains?
Can you help me?

A major part of visiting India is of course, the food. And the good thing is that India is one of the best places to eat gluten free. But make sure you ask what's in the food. Here are some Hindi words and phrases that might come in handy. (Some of these words have been repeated but have been listed to make this section complete.)

Flour – Aata
Wheat – Gehu or Gaihoon
Wheat flour – Maida, Gaihoon ka aata
Food - Khana
Chapatti - Roti
Vegetables – Subjee
Does this food have wheat – Kya iss khanay mei gehu hai
What is it – Ye kya hai

13. Coping with the heat in India

Just when you thought that there wasn't enough to worry about in India, how about the heat? With the help of global warming and India's position on the globe, the country gets temperatures well over 100°F throughout the year. In fact, the city of Delhi had a heat wave in the summer of 2014 that killed over 160 people. These were native people to India as well. To a foreigner that is used to air conditioning and excessive comfort, these temperatures will be even more unbearable. On top of that, tourists that is likely to be overweight or with a series of health problems of their own will need to take extra precautions. If they were to go out under the Indian sun during the summer then they will have an increased chance of getting things like heat stroke, sun burn, dehydration, tropical fatigue, prickly heat and excessive sweating. If you are a tourist under these extremely hot conditions then you have two choices. You can simply stay inside your air conditioned hotel as often as possible or be driven around by a hotel or your holiday company hired taxis (air conditioned if possible) and not auto-rickshaws when you want to go places. However, if you stay inside the hotel then you will be missing out on the experience of seeing India. What would be the point of that? As for these hired taxis, this is a good option but it could be costly after awhile. If you have the money to spend on them, then go for it. Otherwise, you will have to find a way to cope with the heat as you walk around the city you are in.

The girl on the bike has covered her head with her scarf. This serves two purposes. First to shade her head from the heat and secondly to prevent dust getting into her eyes and mouth.

The number one rule when exposing yourself to hot temperatures is to carry lots of bottled water around with you. This means pack your travel bags with bottled water or buy some at the hotel you are staying at. Whenever you get thirsty or you feel dehydrated, just take out the water and drink it to rehydrate yourself. But, don't wait until you are dehydrated to finally hydrate yourself. You should be drinking plenty of water before you even go outside because that will give your body enough of a water reserve to stay hydrated for awhile. Make sure you drink mostly water because this is what naturally hydrates your body. If you drink things like Pepsi or Cola then you are not really going to hydrate your body because those carbonated drinks will make you retain water instead of it being used to hydrate you. As for your food intake, you will want to eat fresh natural foods, such as fruits and vegetables. This might sound like a diet plan for losing weight, but you have to remember that natural foods are what the body needs to stay vital. If you eat a bunch of candy bars and potato chips then your body is going to fatigue quickly when out under the hot Indian sun. Fruit and vegetables will at least give you the essential vitamins and antioxidants your body needs to survive under more extreme temperatures for longer periods of time.

The clothes you wear outside under the sun should be of special consideration. Normally, people want to wear a minimal amount of clothing in hot temperatures because it is more comfortable and they will get a tan. Well, the Indian sun will give you more than just a tan. You will easily get sunburn if you spend more than an hour out in the sun, especially if you have very fair skin. Instead, you should actually wear "cotton" long sleeved shirts or tops. The idea is to cover up as much skin as possible, so that you don't get burned in as many places. This also coincides with the method for preventing mosquitoes from biting you, as discussed in other chapters. As for the rest of your skin, such as your face, you should apply sunscreen on these areas. It will give you about 60% protection from the UV rays, which means it could buy you a little more time outside under the sun. But, don't overdo it.

Always wear sunglasses to cover and protect your eyes. So bring a pair of decent sunglasses with you. If you can, carry a small face towel or handkerchief with you to wipe out the access sweat of your face when you are in the sun. And finally, wear a cap of some kind that will over the face and keep the sun off.

14. Importance of travel insurance in a country like India

Travel insurance is something you should always have when visiting a foreign country, particularly a third world country like India. Earlier in the book, we talked about the importance of travel health insurance because you never know what injuries or illnesses that you might endure when visiting a strange land. Not only are you unfamiliar with the physical dangers, but your body does not have the immunities built up to withstand a lot of the bacteria and disease swarming around the country. Travel health insurance will make sure you are covered for all medical expenses related to health problems you endure during your trip.

Delhi Airport: It's always a good idea to get travel insurance before traveling to India just in case something happened

It is important that you study the different travel insurance packages carefully because they all offer different degrees of help in regards to health and the trip itself. For example, travel insurance can reimburse you on the payments you made if you have to cancel your trip because of an illness or death in the family. You should also get luggage reimbursement coverage because you never know what could happen to your luggage at an Indian airport or during transit. The workers there might not be as professional with your luggage as other developed airports. This might just be speculation, but you should always be ready for anything when it comes to your luggage. I remember one time; I had a handle broken on my suitcase during transit. Luckily, the airline picked up the luggage from my house and had it fixed. Some travel insurance policies will even reimburse you for a luggage delay problem, which is when your luggage isn't available to you for more than 12 hours after you arrive at your destination.

In India, you will definitely want your policy to cover emergency evacuations, which is also called "international evacuation insurance". This is insurance that will pay to have somebody bring you to the nearest medical facility in case you are injured or ill during your trip. In India, there are lots of remote areas where you could run into trouble. As previously discussed, if you were to get bitten by a wild animal then you would need to seek medical attention immediately in order to get tested for rabies. Emergency evacuation will find you and get you to the nearest facility that covers this kind of treatment. Without this insurance, you might find it difficult to get things done. Most evacuation insurance plans will pay up to $1,000,000 to help you evacuate during your medical emergency.

Since India can be a dangerous country at times (which country isn't), you will want to protect yourself as much as possible. The travel health insurance should cover more than just basic medical care needs. If you choose the Accidental Death & Dismemberment option, the insurance company will pay you around $50,000 if you lose a limb or your life during the trip. If you die then the money would go to your family to help pay for funeral expenses. You can also add additional coverage of up to $50,000 for accidental sickness, which would occur if you contracted a disease or bacteria that made you ill.

You might think that it is a little extreme to add all of these extra options, but you don't really know how much your medical care is going to cost. If you get seriously sick with a disease that has no cure then you will need constant medical attention. Between the hospital stay, food, treatments and medicines; you could be looking at hundreds of thousands of dollars in medical expenses. If you don't have enough coverage, you will have to pay that out of your own pocket. Most people don't have that much money saved, so it would likely bankrupt you. That is why you can never have enough medical insurance when you go to a country like India.

15. Quacks or fake doctors in India

There are so many reasons why tourists could run into problems if they get injured or sick in India. Although India has good doctors and clinics but sometimes it can be difficult to find professional medical care in the country, a desperate tourist that needs medical attention might find themselves going to a doctor who is not a real doctor. These kinds of fake doctors are called "quacks." Usually, these quacks are found in poor areas of India where people are desperate for medical attention. They don't have the requisite MBBS degree (bachelor of medicine, bachelor of surgery) required to be a registered doctor.

You will find quacks everywhere. They can do everything from cleaning ears to pulling teeth out. Watch this documentary to learn more about quacks in India.
http://www.shalusharma.net/quacks-india

The quacks don't really do much except take your temperature and then give you antibiotics and other basic medicines. The trouble is that they don't know much. The patients don't know any better and think they're getting quality care. So, they are happy to pay the little money they have in order to get treated. Some quacks even trade organs by taking out the organs of poor patients and giving them to healthy patients. This is illegal, but the Indian government does very little to enforce the law. In fact, there was an anti-quackery bill drawn up amongst Delhi government officials, but nothing ever came of it. The truth is that private medicine practices in India are big business. In fact, India has more fake doctors than they do genuine doctors. The reason why the fake doctors target poor people is because they provide affordable healthcare, whereas the genuine doctors are too expensive for them. As for government run clinics, most of them are too far away for people to get to them. Don't forget that poor Indian people don't have cars and they can't afford transport fares to larger towns and cities for treatment. This leaves them to resort to walking, which would be impossible if they are sick. So, their only alternative is to go to a local quack doctor.

Despite the unqualified aspect of being a quack doctor, they are still quite popular in India. In fact, these doctors don't even try to hide the fact that they are quacks. They admit it and are actually proud of it because they know the Indian government won't do anything to stop them. They also know that they are helping people who have no other options. Unfortunately, there are some quacks that try to do more than just take your temperature and give you a pill. If they try to diagnosis a particular kind of illness, they can most often be wrong about the diagnosis. All they will do is prescribe steroids in order to give the patient a pick-me-up and then supply more outdated antibiotics. These antibiotics are what most quack doctors prescribe without really knowing if they are necessary for the patient. This could affect the patient negatively in the future because their bodies will develop a resistance to the antibiotics. So, when the day comes that they need to get antibiotics, they won't work in their system.

Remember these quacks are of three basic categories;

(a) Those who do not have any qualifications whatsoever – the most dangerous types.

(b) Those practitioners of traditional Indian Medicine namely Ayurvedic, Homeopathy and Naturopathy (called Ayush) but illegally practice modern medicine as well.

(c) Those practitioners of integrated medicine or alternative systems of medicine. Some names of these practice include electro-homeopathy, indo-allopathy etc.

What does all of this mean for a tourist? It means that if you needed a doctor then look for a proper medical center and stay away from a quack. Ayurvedic medicine is a form of alternative medicine which has been used for centuries in India and is fine as long as it's taken with conventional medicine.

There is something called "medical tourism" that foreigners can take advantage of. These are government and private clinics run facilities where foreign tourists can go to receive medical care. The idea behind this was due to the increasing amount of healthcare costs in other countries, like the United States. Medical tourism is meant to be an option for Americans and others around the world because they can go to India for affordable medical treatment. This is the best option even if you are a real tourist of India and happen to fall ill or get injured.

If you have travel health insurance then you know that you will be safe in India as far as health is concerned. Find out from your insurance carrier prior to leaving for India.

16. Waterborne diseases in India

When you come from a developed country it is easy to take fresh water for granted. You have it in your sinks and even in your toilets. It is not 100% purified, but it is tested and filtered for all possible diseases that could exist. Not only that, some countries also have purified drinking water sold in bottles. Unfortunately, the people of India do not have this luxury. Even though there are a lot of Indian cities with a vast water supply, the management of the water is not as good. The citizens don't just go to the supermarket to buy water as much as in Western countries.

In some villages of India, even today, it is the job of women to source out water for their families by getting it from the waterways that flow in their communities. Sometimes it gets collected from rivers or lakes that can be dirty. This is how waterborne diseases come into existence in India. These diseases include cholera, Japanese Encephalitis, filariasis, typhoid, malaria and diarrhea. Since this water is not managed properly, the diseases spread very fast amongst the people and cause a lot of death. Sometimes this is even due to sewage flowing into the water supply and contaminating it. The Indian government to be honest does not do much to stop the water from getting polluted, so it is up to the citizens to take care of it themselves. People in the cities and towns boil their drinking water even if it comes from the water supply pipes.

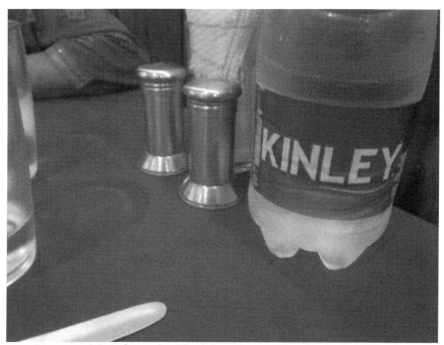
Always drink from bottled (packaged) water at all times

Tourists need to drink bottled water whenever possible. This point has been emphasized a lot in this book, but that is because there are so many diseases that exist in the Indian water supply. Cholera is a disease that can kill you within hours after ingesting it through water. As for diarrhea, it is not fatal but it can leave you feeling dehydrated for 2 weeks. Typhoid is also not fatal, but will leave you feeling sleepy and feverish. Filariasis is nothing but a parasitic disease that usually affects people that live near contaminated water bodies. If you are a tourist then you won't have to worry much about this one. Malaria is a disease discussed in another chapter in this book. Basically, mosquitoes that carry malaria will nest near water bodies and pollute the water with the disease just from being there. The point to all of this is that you should try to stay away from man-made stagnant water bodies in India.

If you are unable to get bottled water in India for whatever reason, then you will have no choice but to resort to regular

Indian water. You may be able to trust the water you get from a major hotel or restaurant, but it is better to be safe than sorry. What you should do is bring a portable water purifier with you. Also, iodine tablets will help disinfect the water from diseases.

However, the best solution that can be mixed with the other treatments is boiling water. Now this might be hard to do if you are a tourist because where are you going to get a stove to boil water on? You could always buy a portable stove as well, but you have to make sure you can plug it in somewhere unless it runs on batteries. If you boil water to 212°F then it will kill the bacteria that exist in the water. This is an extreme solution that you can do if you are worried about the water and have no more bottled water available. Chances are the restaurants and hotels will perform a similar function on their water. It may be a good idea to sneak into the kitchen and see how they actually purify their water. This might sound like a crazy idea, but it is about your health so it is worth it.

17. Bird Flu in India and how to avoid it

Bird flu is an infectious disease that could be fatal to humans if left untreated. Even though the Indian government recently said they were free of bird flu, this could have just been a political claim with no merit behind it. You should take caution when going to India by understanding where bird flu lies. It is mostly found in Indian poultry such as ducks and chickens. Sometimes pigs and humans may get it, but this is less likely. The bird flu spreads when birds come in contact with other infected birds or their feces. This causes them to get infected themselves. As for humans, they don't even have to eat the poultry to contract this virus. They could just step near a bird that has it and contract it. You will know when you have the virus because you will have symptoms like fever, coughing, muscle aches, abdominal pains, breathing difficulty and sore throat. There are also no vaccines that can prevent the virus from infecting you. All you can do is take preventative action to avoid getting it all together. You could take some antiviral drugs before going to India, but they are not specifically made for the bird flu. However, it could help reduce your chances of getting it. The two most recommended prescription drugs for this are zanamivir and oseltamivir. Ask your doctor about them at least a few weeks before going to India.

It should not be hard for a tourist to avoid getting the bird flu. Unless they are going to India to farm poultry, they will be pretty safe. Tourists just have to be careful not to go to any farms or agricultural buildings. As for eating poultry, you just have to remember not to eat anything raw. This means no drinking raw eggs from a glass to get a quick boost of energy. You need to cook your eggs and your chicken when you eat them, or make sure somebody else cooks them. If the food is cooked at 70°C for 30 minutes then it will kill any bird flu that exists and it will be safe to eat. It may get tricky when you eat at Indian restaurants because you have to depend on someone else to cook the poultry properly. This is another reason why you should not eat at a small restaurant with few people because it may not be very healthy. Chances are if you eat at the bigger restaurants of your hotel then you will be safe.

There is also another big problem surrounding bird flu, which is the fact that you can get it from another person that is carrying it. Bird flu is contagious, so you must be sanitary around people as often as possible. This means washing your hands thoroughly with soap before and after you eat a meal. If you shake anyone's hand that you do not know, then you should wash your hands immediately afterwards. It may seem dramatic but it's better to be safe than sorry.

If you happen to walk near live poultry then it wouldn't hurt to wear a mask or covering your face. Since the pollution in some Indian cities might prompt you to does this, these masks will now serve multiple purposes as well.

Bird flu is not commonly caught by tourists, so this should be the least of your worries when going to India. If you can just remember to take caution around poultry and food derived from poultry, then you should be fine.

Always wash your hands and stay as sanitary as possible.

18. Garbage on the side of the road

It is great to live in a country that has regular garbage pickup. It is even better when city workers are paid to go around and pick up garbage off the ground that is polluting the environment. Indian towns and cities also have this service but often they are not implemented by the authorities. As a tourist, you will see a lot of garbage and debris on the side of the road that just gets left there till the municipal authorities take them away. People will litter and throw their trash out onto the streets without taking into account the environmental damage it is doing. However, the real source of the problem has to do with the Municipal Solid Waste Management Rules not being enforced by the government. These are rules that are supposed to protect Indian citizens from unsanitary conditions caused by excess garbage buildup. Instead, these rules go ignored and the health of the people is put in jeopardy. City streets can be covered with filth, which eventually ends up in the waterways where people drink out of. Each day in India, there is over hundreds of children who get sick because their drinking water is contaminated from garbage buildup.

Garbage on the road is an issue in many towns and cities of India. It attracts animals and is a breeding ground for rats and mice.

You will often see people picking dry waste such as plastic at these dumps which they sell to plants that recycle them. Some cities such as Bangalore are able to manage their waste quite nicely but in many other cities of India, this garbage problem has reached a tipping point. Another issue is that if garbage continues to be dumped, contaminated water reaches the ground water and pollutes the drinking water source which is hazardous to health.

Another statistic shows that large sections of the Indian population suffer from some kind of disease due to this pollution. This is a pretty serious when you consider that 1/5 of the world's population lives in India. The whole country produces over 200 million tons of waste per year, and they don't know where to put it all. So obviously, something has to be done about this or else millions of more people are going to die.

As a tourist, what does the garbage problem mean for you? For one thing, it is surely an extra incentive to drink bottled water as opposed to water served in a glass. When you walk on the streets of India, try to avoid touching the garbage with your hands or exposing it to your skin. You don't know what kind of diseases or parasites maybe inhabiting the garbage. The amount of garbage you will see depends on where you go, but chances are you will see lots of it when you are in a towns and cities even in a place like Agra (the place where Taj Mahal is situated).

This is supposed to be a rubbish bin but people decided to throw litter outside it for some reason

In fact, Indian tourism has been down because of all the pollution from the garbage. Not only is it unhealthy to be around, but it is not appealing to look at either. Nobody wants to fly for 18 hours across the world and then land on a garbage dump. I have heard many tourists saying that they liked India but they did not like the dirt and filth that was all around them.

On top of that, you have the air pollution problems in some cities as well. All you can do is either go to a rural area or rub lots of antibacterial cream on your skin. If you go to a rural area then you have the other problems discussed in this book, like wild animals biting you. In the touristy areas, there are plenty of shopping centers and reputable restaurants you can visit. Once inside these places, you might forget that you are even in a location that has so much garbage outside. It will make your trip better and healthier by simply staying away from the garbage. That is really all you can do because no one is going to clean it up for you.

Not all is gloom and doom about the garbage situation. India is currently devising a way to turn garbage into fuel. The city of Delhi has already installed two incinerators that will be able to turn the city's garbage into electrical energy. This is still in the experimental stages, but once this happens it could very well be the turning point for the garbage problem in the city and in the rest of the country.

All in all, try not to worry too much about it. If you see rubbish dump just go past it and nothing should happen.

19. Packing list for India

India is a developing country, but they are still very conservative when it comes to their dress codes. Although you can find almost everything that you would want but nonetheless, it is imperative that you pack the right items and supplies before departing, so that you can stay safe and protect yourself. The first thing you need to look at his your luggage itself. If you are taking a long trip to India and are bringing a lot of items, then you will want to bring a suitcase. However, the roads of India can be dusty and have pot holes so be prepared for that if you plan to wheel your suitcase around many streets. If you are traveling light and plan to do a lot of walking, then a backpack will suit you just fine. As for your clothes, you should pack long sleeved shirts and pants made of cotton. People may dress more westernized in Delhi or Mumbai, but the smaller towns and villages stick to conservative dress standards. You should cover up as much skin as you can. Indian women wear something called the "dupatta" to cover the contours of their chest. Women could pack scarves to wear around their neck and chest area, or else it will give Indian men the wrong idea. You can always buy one when in India.

Make sure you bring everything you need in India especially medicines

The one item you should pay close attention to is a personal medical kit. Even though you may have travel insurance to cover medical costs, you may still need immediate medical attention if you are somewhere in India that is far away from people. A personal medical kit should be filled with the right medicines and antiseptic medications that can temporarily treat wounds and fever symptoms. On the top of the list should be antibacterial cream, like Mupirocin. This will help kill any bacteria that may get on your skin. You should also pack antibiotics if you can, such as cephalexin, because skin infections are very common in India and you may forget to use your antibacterial cream one day.

Some other items you will need are insect repellent with DEET, Ibuprofen, sun block, bandages and iodine tablets even though you may not need them. Many of these items were talked about in other chapters. The repellent wards off mosquitoes, ibuprofen helps reduce fever symptoms in case you contract an illness and then iodine tablets can help purify water. These are only preventive care items, but don't go crazy and think they are going to keep you 100% safe. Always use caution when drinking water or going outside.

The most important items to pack are your passport and travel insurance information. These two things are important in case you run into problems in India, such as obtaining an illness or injury. It could also come in handy if you need to visit your embassy in an emergency situation. Without them, you could be stuck in India until your information can be verified. This could take weeks, so you certainly won't want that to happen. Overall, you don't need to pack heavy for your trip to India. All you need are a few changes of clothes, passport, driver's license, insurance information and basic medical kit. You can optionally choose to bring bottled water and canned food if you truly don't trust the Indian restaurants to be sanitary. But I don't recommend it as one of the charms of India is its food.

If you are good at consolidating then you should be able to pack most of this into one suitcase. The ID and paperwork should be packed into a carryon bag because you don't want to risk your suitcase being lost and then having no way to claim it, or even prove who you are. This means one suitcase and one carryon bag should be sufficed for the trip.
Women might consider bring some female urinary devices. Some of the public toilets in India is horrendous and these devices lets women urinate while standing up.

Here's a comprehensive list of travel items for India:
http://www.shalusharma.com/essential-travel-items-for-india

20. Insect bites and stings in India

India has a very tropical climate, which means there are a variety of bugs and insects that one will have to watch out for. India is no stranger to dangerous insects, like scorpions, ticks, bedbugs, mosquitoes, bees, spiders and even flies. People don't typically worry about insects biting them all that much. The worst that usually happens from a bite is that it leaves a rash or causes some minor itching. But, you have to remember that bugs in India are a lot more dangerous than bugs in other parts of the world. As you already know from reading this book, mosquitoes can carry diseases and parasites in them.

Scorpions are present in mostly rural areas hiding particularly in corners and under rubble. So be extra careful if you are planning to stay in rural India

As for the other bugs that sting and bite, they won't typically give you a disease. Instead, they will give you a much more excessive irritation then you are probably used to back home. These irritations could include swelling, redness, burning, numbness, weakness and breathlessness. Some of these bugs may even carry bacteria that will make you sick, but it won't be in the depths of a disease. It is important to know how to prevent and treat these attacks when they occur. You could even risk death by being around these insects. If you get stung by a Black Indian Scorpion then it will release toxins into your bloodstream, which are fatal. Word to the wise; avoid all scorpions and spiders whenever you can. Unlike some spiders in Western countries, spiders in India are best avoided as many of the species found in India are poisonous.

As for most insects that sting you, the result will just be a feeling of numbness in the part that was stung. However, you may still get an infection so you have to take proper measures to clean it out. The first thing you should do if you get stung is not panic. Next, find a straight edged object and remove the stinger that still resides in your skin. After the stinger is out, wash the wound with purified water and soap. Then put ice in a cloth and press it against the stung area. If you have any antihistamines then take those as well. Most things that sting you, like bees and small scorpions, will just leave you feeling numb for awhile. The numbness will eventually wear off, but cleaning the wound will prevent infection. When it comes to bed bugs, they will just chew your skin while you sleep. But, their bites can also make you sick if left untreated. The best way to prevent getting bitten is to spray your bed with simple bug spray. Make sure the spray does not irritate the skin because you will have to sleep on that bed.

When you go out around town in India, try to use insect repellent spray on your skin. This will greatly prevent nasty bugs from biting you unexpectedly. Of course, there is no way to completely avoid getting bit because bugs pop up in all kinds of places, even hotel rooms. The best way to prevent dealing with bugs indoors is to not leave any food or trash lying around. The reason why the outdoors has so many bugs in India is because of all the garbage buildup much of it will be outside. If you have a clean hotel room then you should be able to avoid them for the most part, except for the bed bugs. They thrive on human blood, so make sure you spray down your bed good with bug spray. Besides that, try to walk around with your personal medical kit wherever you go. If you are outdoors somewhere far from town and you get bit, you will want to have the necessary supplies available to treat the wound before you get an infection.

Good hotels and guest houses no matter how basic will clean and make sure there are no insects in the room

Some places are infested with ants. Good hotels and guest houses will make sure that they disinfect the floor and make sure that the rooms are ants-free. If you do find lots of ants then ask them to disinfect the room so that the rooms become free of insects. Mind you the insects in India are a nuisances and they can bite particularly the red ones (Solenopsis invicta). If you do get bitten by these ants then wash affected area with soap and water and apply some hand sanitizer.

Cockroaches are too a big issues in Indian homes. If the floors are not kept clean then soon there will be plenty of them running around especially in the kitchen and the worst thing is that they do harbor disease carrying causing bacteria. Hopefully you will not encounter them in hotels. Again if you did get bitten by them then wash the area with soap and water and use a disinfectant.

21. Tips for women traveling to India

Women travelers going to India will face some special challenges because of their gender. You have to remember that the westernized part of the world treats women differently than the eastern part, especially the lesser developed countries like India. Women are expected to dress conservatively. In other words, women who dress in revealing clothes will be seen as provocative to the Indian people. The native Indian women wear lots of clothing to cover up any part of themselves that would be a sexual turn on towards a man. So, when foreign women come to India and wear shorts or a tight t-shirt, then they are likely prone to getting sexually harassed or something called "eve teasing" (a term used by Indians for sexual harassment, molestation or groping) by Indian men. Usually, the harassment is in the form of lewd verbal comments, but sometimes men might actually grope a woman if they are close enough. This also has to do with the westernized culture of Hollywood movies that represent women in a sexually provocative way. Indian men see these movies and automatically assume that all women from the west act like that. Female tourists really have to be on their guard and cover up as much as possible.

Women should wear modestly and cover up as much as possible

India is not a country with a lot of proper plumbing, especially with bathrooms. If you go into a typical public bathroom you will see a toilet that will look like a hole in the ground – these are squat toilets. This is where both men and women go to urinate. It may be easy for a man to urinate because he releases urine through his penis. As for a woman who has not used these types of toilets before, she will need a little help when it comes to urinating in them. Unless she wants to squat all the way down onto the ground, she will need a female urination device that will allow her to aim just like a man. If you are a female thinking about traveling to India then make sure you get one of these devices. It is basically a cylindrical funnel that goes inside of you and lets you control where your urine goes. This allows women to urinate while standing up just like a man. That way, females won't have to drop their pants and risk getting a disease from being near the filthy floor of the bathroom.

A public toilet in India. Women might find it easier if they used a female urination device in toilets like these

Another thing that women will want to bring with them is tampons. India does sell tampons, but they are actually in limited supply. In fact, Delhi recently announced that they were completely out of tampons in the marketplace. So, tourists shouldn't depend on buying them in India for this reason.

Some people would advise women not to travel alone when they are in India. Although nothing wrong with it and in fact a lot of foreign women travel to India along. But it does help to be in the company of at least one man for nothing more than protection. Some men may seek an opportunity to assault a foreign woman, either sexually or simply to rob her. If a man is by her side then this is less likely to happen although we all know that there are no guarantees about anything.

Connaught Place in New Delhi is very popular amongst foreign and local tourists

You have to remember that women in India sometimes are not treated properly and India is still a country where a lot of sexual crimes happen. Therefore, this goes for female tourists as well. If a woman presents herself as independent by walking alone, then she may be vulnerable to abuse. A man that is with her will indicate to others that she is his "property," so to speak. If a woman can travel with multiple men then it is even better.

Indian men are not all bad though – most are nice people as in most parts of the world. It's usually the criminally minded men who will take desperate actions when the opportunity presents itself. For the most part, women will be safe as long as they try to adapt to the culture and not act too westernized. This will show respect to the people of India and they will admire that.

22. Is meat safe in India?

As a tourist, it is important that you understand the culture of India and how they typically eat. When it comes to cooking the meat of an animal, this is often seen as an art form rather than a cuisine. Many Indian people are vegetarians and do not even touch or like the sight of meat. That's not to say that they don't have cooked meat available to eat because they do.

Some of the best Indians foods are non-vegetarian particularly lamb, chicken and fish preparations. The point is that the meat may not have been cooked thoroughly enough or in a sanitary environment. This book has already strongly advised against going to a small time Indian restaurant. Avoiding meat is definitely one of those reasons because it has to be cooked just right in order to prevent any possible stomach issues out of it. Street vendors and roadside eateries are definitely places you don't want to eat meat from. Also, stay away from pork because pigs are the most diseased animal in India. Most restaurants in India won't be serving any pork or beef due to Hindus not eating beef and Muslims not eating pork. Mind you, in places like Goa you will find both types of meat being served in restaurants.

You should take a decision there and then if you want to try meat and poultry dishes in India

Tourists should just follow everyone else. You should only eat at restaurants that have a lot of people in them, both tourists and locals. Chances are these restaurants are serving quality meat or else everyone would be getting sick and complaining about the food. These restaurants are also used to adapting to more westernized dishes, like steak and chicken. They even serve meat kebabs on a stick as well. If you can find restaurants that import their meat then go with those first. Part of the reason why Indian meat makes people sick is because of the conditions that the poultry and cattle are raised in. For example, goats are often just tied up right outside the butcher's shop and are fed whatever leftovers the butcher can get his hands on, like vegetable scraps and garbage. As for poultry, the chickens are kept in very tiny cages where feces build up fast. On top of that, there are no antibiotics or pesticides used on the birds under these terrible conditions. If most foreigners saw what the living conditions of these animals were like, they would probably never want to eat meat in India again. That is why if you can find a restaurant that uses imported meat, then chances are it is worth eating. Of course, it will likely be more expensive as well. This doesn't mean that all Indian meat are bad quality, it's just that you don't know where they are coming from.

There may be safe places to eat meat in India, but the risk of getting sick could be high. This is especially true for the fish meat that is served. Fish is a delicacy in India, but it is something that spoils very fast. Many Indian restaurants claim to serve fresh fish, but often times it is not fresh and might give you food poisoning. That is why you should avoid all fish because it is the number one kind of meat that causes people to get sick in India. To be on the safe side, you should just avoid meat all together. The whole point of going to India is to try and adapt to the culture. If you become a temporary vegetarian and eat the foods that locals usually eat, then you will get a better cultural experience of their cuisine. But, if you are persistent on eating meat then you might want to think about bringing canned meat with you. This could be canned tuna fish, salmon or baby shrimps. Even though it doesn't taste as good, you could mix it with the vegetarian meals you get in India and create a whole new dish for yourself. Then you could have the peace of mind of knowing that you have safe meat and Indian cuisine to eat.

Mind you, there are MacDonald's and other major outlets that serve the same thing you will have in your own country and the way they cook it will more or less be the same. In addition, you can assure that the quality of the meat will be good.

MacDonald's in India

So, is meat safe in India? The safe answer to this question would be "yes and no" at the same time. Yes, if the restaurant is reputed and has visibly a lot of people in it. No, when you aren't sure what the source of meat is and there aren't many people in a particular eatery. Just be careful and judge for yourself.

23. Useful health Hindi words and phrases

Most people in the travel industry will be able to communicate in English to some extent but nonetheless, here are some health words and phrases that you could use if required. Remember you will only be able to use Hindi in North India.

Most people will be able to understand English however some people will not know English whatsoever – For example, like this woman selling tea

Health – Tabiyat
How's your health – Aap ki tabiyat kai-see hai
My health is not good – Mari tabiyat acchee nahi hai
Stomach – Pate or Pait
Pain – Dard
I am in pain – Mujhe dard hai, Mai dard mai hu
My stomach is hurting – Mera pate dard kar raha hai
Doctor – Doctor

I need a doctor – Mujhe ek doctor chahiye
Where can I find a doctor – Doctor kaha meelayga
Water – Paani
Where is the water from? – Paani kaha say sai?
I need bottled water - Mujhe bottled pani chahiye
Which bottled water do you have? – App ke pass kaun ka bottled water hai?
I need a bottle of Bisleri? - Mujhe chahiye?
Dirty – Ganda
This is dirty – Ye ganda hai
Clean - Saaf
Is this food clean? – Kya ye khana saaf hai?
This glass is dirty – Ye glass dirty hai
Medicine – Dawa
I need a bandage – Mujhe bandage chaheeye
Painkillers - Dard ki goliya
Cough – Khasee
I need cough medicines – Mujhe khasee ki dawa chaiye
I need my medicines – Mujhe meri dawa chahiye
Sick – Beemar
I am sick – Mai beemar hu
Cold – Sardee, Jukaam
Mujhe cold hai – Mujhe sardee (jukaam) hai
Soap – Sabun
Where is the soap – Sabun kaha hai
Hospital – Haspataal (Hospital will also do)
Shop – Dukaan
Pharmacy or medicine shop – Dawa kee dukaan, Dawa-khana
Where is the hospital – Haspataal kaha hai
Fever – Bhukhar
I have a fever – Mujhe fever hai
I don't feel well – Mai accha nahi "feel" kar raha hu (male); Mai accha nahi "feel" kar rahee hu (female)
Choke – Dum ghutna
I am choking – Mara dum ghut raha hai
Urine – Paysaab
Blood – Khoon, Rakt
Blood test – Rakt jaanch, Khoon jaanch
Disease – Rog

Headache – Sardard
I have a headache – Mujhe sardard hai
Allergy – Allergy (used in Hindi)
I have an allergy – Mujhe allergy hai
Wheat - Geyhu
I have an allergy to wheat –Mujhe allergy hai geyhu say

24. Message from the author

You have made it to the end of the book. Hopefully, you now have a clear picture about what to expect when traveling to India. Even though there are many historic sites and tourist attractions to visit while you are there, it doesn't mean that you won't have bad experiences as well. This book was not meant to scare you, but rather to open your mind to the truth about health implications while traveling in India. Despite the attractions, it is still a third world country with disease, poverty and crime. If you stay in the central touristy areas then chances are you won't run into too many problems with these things.

Most tourists coming to India are fine and never encounter any issues. If most major hotels of India were not sanitary then tourists would get sick immediately and it would deter them from ever coming back to the country. But nonetheless, it is up to the tourists themselves to take preventive measures, so that they don't end up with disease, or stomach upset or any other health issues that could make them severely sick or possibly take their life. All it takes is one small slip up or bad assumption for this to happen to you.

If you take anything away from this book, it should be the emphasis on preparing for a healthy journey to India and avoiding all the possible problems you could face. The information in this book has shown you the diseases that exist in the country as well as the sanitary concerns that you should have while eating there. Before even going to India, you need to make sure you have all of your vaccinations to protect yourself from the various diseases that you may encounter there. Also, remember to pack the right supplies for your trip, like repellents, long clothing, your medicines and medical kits. You need to cover all possible problems that could occur while in India because there are many.

Since India is a poor country, the vendors there will cut any corner in order to make a buck. They don't take into account the health of their customers. All they care about are profits, which is why the business of being a quack doctor is so lucrative there. The Indian government has some health regulations, but they often don't enforce them like they do in the United States. It is up to the tourist to watch their own back and to keep themselves safe and healthy. Hopefully, you will use the information from this book to do just that. If you have any further questions about the risks involved with traveling to India, then you should contact the Center for Disease Control or your local doctor and ask questions about what to expect in India. Then you can work with them to figure out the best possible solutions for protecting yourself.

Thank you for purchasing this book. It was written with your health and safety in mind. Now enjoy your trip to India and remember to stay safe!

If you have any questions on India or travelling to India, then feel free to ask me a question on my website http://www.shalusharma.com and feel free to subscribe to my newsletter for travel related news on India http://www.shalusharma.com/subscribe. I will try my best to answer any questions that you might have.

Here are my other books that you might consider buying:

India Travel Survival Guide For Women - ISBN-10: 149122648X
Essential Hindi Words And Phrases For Travelers To India - ISBN-10: 1492752517
Hinduism For Kids: Beliefs And Practices - ISBN-10: 1495370429
India For Kids: Amazing Facts About India - ISBN-10: 149470997X

Best wishes to you and have a nice and safe trip to India.
Feel free to shoot me an email if you want any help.

Take care... Shalu Sharma

Printed in Great Britain
by Amazon